Winner of the L. E. Phillabaum Poetry Award for 2005

OTHER BOOKS BY MARILYN NELSON

A Wreath for Emmett Till (2005), by Marilyn Nelson,
illustrated by Phillipe Lardy

Fortune's Bones: The Manumission Requiem (2004),
by Marilyn Nelson

Carver: A Life in Poems (2001), by Marilyn Nelson

Triolets for Triolet (2001), by Marilyn Nelson

She-Devil Circus (2001), by Marilyn Nelson

The Fields of Praise: New and Selected Poems (1997),
by Marilyn Nelson

Magnificat (1994), by Marilyn Nelson Waniek

Partial Truth (1992), by Marilyn Nelson Waniek

The Homeplace (1990), by Marilyn Nelson Waniek

Mama's Promises (1985), by Marilyn Nelson Waniek

*The Cat Walked Through the Casserole and Other
Poems for Children* (1984), by Pamela Espeland and
Marilyn Waniek

*Hundreds of Hens and Other Poems for Children by
Halfdan Rasmussen* (1982), translated from the Dan-
ish by Marilyn Nelson Waniek and Pamela Espeland

For the Body (1978), by Marilyn Nelson Waniek

The Cachoeira Tales and Other Poems

Marilyn Nelson

Louisiana State University Press
Baton Rouge

Published by Louisiana State University Press
Copyright © 2005 by Marilyn Nelson
All rights reserved
Manufactured in the United States of America

Designer: Amanda McDonald Scallan
Typeface: Sabon

Library of Congress Cataloging-in-Publication Data
Nelson, Marilyn, 1946-
   The Cachoeira tales, and other poems / Marilyn Nelson.
      p. cm.
   ISBN 0-8071-3063-X (cloth : alk. paper) — ISBN 0-8071-3064-8 (pbk.
: alk. paper)
   I. Title.
PS3573.A4795C33 2005
811'.54—dc22   2004022420

ISBN 978-0-8071-4310-0 (pdf) — ISBN 978-0-8071-4311-7 (epub) —
ISBN 978-0-8071-4312-4 (mobi)

The author gratefully acknowledges the editors of the following publica-
tions, in which some of the poems first appeared: *Gettysburg Review*
("Faster Than Life") and *Southern Review* (excerpts from *The Cachoeira
Tales*). She also gratefully acknowledges Curbstone Press, which originally
published "Triolets for Triolet" as a limited-edition chapbook.

The author wishes to thank the J. S. Guggenheim Memorial Foundation for
the grant, which made this book possible, and the University of Delaware
for freeing her from teaching duties for a year. She would also like to thank
her fellow "pilgrims," who graciously allowed her to use them as models:
Mercedes Arnold, Jennifer Nelson, Mel Nelson, Albert J. Price Jr., and
Jacob Wilkenfeld. Thanks again to Pamela Espeland, editor and friend.

The paper in this book meets the guidelines for permanence and durability
of the Committee on Production Guidelines for Book Longevity of the
Council on Library Resources. ∞

Contents

The Cachoeira Tales and Other Poems

Faster Than Light

for Ohio Wesleyan University Chapter
Phi Beta Kappa, Eta of Ohio, 2002

I didn't want to pay to park my car,
so I took a taxi to the train station.
New London is an hour's drive away,
but it was the best solution I could find.
After ten miles or so of idle chat
in which my occupation was confessed,
the driver said *he* was a physicist—
As a hobby, he said: Driving was his trade.
Still struggling to connect my seat-belt clasp,
I asked his opinion of an article
I'd skimmed last weekend in the *New York Times,*
about a man who researches time travel.

He made that *pffft* Parisian cabbies make
in early August, when Americans
try to *parlez avec* them at rush hour.
He gave me a long over-the-shoulder glare,
squeezed the steering wheel, and hit the gas.
He said, *He's wrong. The one thing that would work
is to fly faster than the speed of light,
through a wormhole. The gravitational field
is full of holes: You only have to find
one and be pulled by metagravitational force.
For energy you could use compressed song . . .*
(or words to that effect. My memory

isn't what it was ten minutes ago).
He drove with ten white knuckles on the wheel,
his pinched blue right eye looking back at me,
as we took the curves on two screaming tires.
*Faster than light travel, that's the secret.
The government's been onto this for years.
There are other planets waiting to be explored.*

This one's almost used up; it's time to move.
We won't take people who don't measure up,
our intellectual inferiors.
Let them inherit the earth: We'll take the skies.
(I still couldn't figure out the seat-belt catch.)

The poor and ignorant population grows
so quickly . . . What?! Deny the right to life?
There's a fuckin' holocaust of the unborn!
But some races and cultures lack the gift
of scientific knowledge. It's the dross
of their stupidity which weighs us down
and holds us back. Faster than light travel!
Faster than light travel! The only way!
We hurtled down the turnpike, passing trucks
Faster than light! and cars full of people
driving hell-bent to get to work on time.
Faster than light travel, that's the ticket!

Finally, we pulled up at the train station.
(I'd given up on fastening my seat belt—
stupid contraption—trusting to
the universe to grant me more good luck.)
I scrambled out. We wished each other well.
(My tip was generous, if I do say so myself.)
Faster than light, he yelled, late for his next
pickup, zooming off, talking to his phone.
(My cup brimmed over with Psalm Twenty-Three.
Buoyancy's sometimes stronger than gravity.)
I wheeled my luggage down the crowded train,
then found a seat and opened my magazine.

Some influence is affecting a space probe,
I read, which baffles scientists. It will
rewrite the laws of physics and astronomy
when scientists understand and name that force.
The plan was for *Pioneer 10* to arrive

some million years from now, at some far place.
In case of alien contact, there's a plaque
of a human couple, and a celestial map
showing Earth with a spear held to her head.
Thirty years beyond its launch, it's past Pluto,
the farthest planet orbiting our sun,
in empty space 7 billion miles from Earth.

The article said current theories can't explain
what's causing the decrease in *Pioneer*'s speed.
It's almost imperceptible, a mere
6 mph per century: But *Pioneer 10*
is being pulled back to the sun. I closed my eyes.
. . . *Several million years from now.* As if
a species on the brink of extinguishing itself
said to a future species, *Remember me?*
The species which perfected genocide?
Will Science ever discover humility?
Right, Fool: You want to say en garde *to Science?*
Why stop there? Why don't you attack Knowledge,

while you're at it? And how about Progress?
Ain't that a bit ambitious, Miss William Blake?
What was that voice? Listen, Marilyn, listen:
as saints once listened (and, of course, the mad).
I looked around: The other passengers
were busy with laptops, breakfasts, books.
And where does it get off, accusing me? Ambition?
Why, I've surpassed every fantasy I had.
Would I presume to bad-mouth our attempt
to cheat death? My poems: a handful of dust
trying to get back to supernova.
Like every longing, everything alive.

But ambition wants the immortality
of a members-only country club Valhalla,
an eternal summit meeting of great names.

Millions of light-years into the future,
that immortality ambition breeds
with serendipity: what will it mean?
Our poetry, our books, our language: dust
of words never again to be spoken.
I wonder what *will* last millions of years:
A stone? A nuclear waste storage site?
Will Homo sapiens evolve, or die?
Will wiser beings populate our Earth?

We're dying faster than the speed of light,
our fame forgettable. Will good deeds, too,
vanish like molecules of exhaled breath,
to be recycled by the universe?
Girl, get on back to the raft. When you try to think,
the breeze between your ears nearly blows me away.
My Muse again. So much for my magazine.
I closed its pages and began to drift.
As if you wasn't drifting all along.
If you had the good sense God promised the carrot,
you'd know that what lasts is the hush of space:
the hiss of orbit, and the hum of stars.

If you could launch a space probe, I wondered,
would you take up my name engraved in gold?
My puny thoughts? My hopes for the future?
And, if I knew I'd be anonymous,
would I publish? Would I write poems at all?
(During the countdown of The Anonymous,
you'd be trying to scratch your initials on the hull.)
Well, Muse of Disposable Poetry,
at least I'm not producing toxic waste!
But poets who want immortality,
poets who are ambitious: Is it wrong
to want life after our deaths for our songs?

Leave immortality to cancer cells:
They don't know when to stop. Just when they reach
the point of no return, the body dies,
and the cancer is returned to genesis.
Genes are programmed to reproduce and die;
and poetry, to stick on a synapse,
lucky to be a line remembered wrong.
Your work, projected into the future,
is pulled back to earth by dark energy,
the glue which binds the cosmos together . . .
From Stamford I no longer traveled alone;
my seatmate fast-talked into his cell phone.

Triolets for Triolet

Triolet: French. An eight-line syllabic stanza turning on two rhymes and built on two refrains. It rhymes ABaAabAB (with A and B standing for the refrains). Its lines may be of any single length. I've slightly modified the form of these triolets.

I got to know the people of a Creole village called Triolet during a visit to the Indian Ocean island nation of Mauritius in 1999. As Creoles—mixed people with African blood—they are at the bottom of their social and economic scale. Their language, French Creole, though spoken by everyone in their small country, is, for those who speak only Creole, a marker of lower-class status. A few months before my visit, the village of Triolet was firebombed in the night, in an act of racist violence. Eighteen houses and a school were destroyed. I spent a lot of time in Triolet during my visit. As the villagers and I exchanged smiles, theirs shyly respectful of the rich black university professor from a distant world they could not dream of ever being able to visit, I felt both our differences and our affinity, as descendants of African slaves.

There are villages like Triolet on islands all over the world. Their inhabitants range through the same beautiful spectrum of browns, and suffer the same poverty, the same indignities, the same inherited shame. By coincidence, I discovered the poetic form just as I decided to try to do something to raise money to help Triolet rebuild. The proceeds from the sale of a limited edition chapbook (three hundred numbered copies published by Curbstone Press) of these triolets were donated to a literacy program there. These triolets are for Triolets everywhere.

M. N.

I begin to suffer from not being a white man . . .

. . . a Negro is forever in combat with his own image.

*I have barely opened eyes that had been blindfolded, and someone
already wants to drown me in the universal? What about the others?
Those who "have no voice," those who "have no spokesman" . . . I
need to lose myself in my negritude, to see the fires, the segregations,
the rapes, the boycotts. We need to put our fingers on every sore that
mottles the black uniform.*

Franz Fanon, *Black Skin, White Masks* (1952)

ONE

Walk through the winding streets of Triolet,
its two-room cement houses, whose tin roofs
seem one bright blaze from satellites miles away.
Walk through the winding streets of Triolet:
Watch as dust rises over children's play.
Maids and cane-cutters come home here to laugh.
Walk through the winding streets of Triolet,
who see you, too. Who know you steal their life.

TWO

Trying to stop, screeching toward Triolet,
the Twentieth Century Express.
. . . A deaf child, lost in reverie or play . . .
Trying to stop, screaming toward Triolet,
your selfishness. Or *ours*. For, I must say,
I'm the Fisherman's Wife, wishing excess.
. . . Wheels sparking, screeching toward Triolet . . .
We hear it, gorging on food we don't bless.

THREE

Without a history, people stumble
around the grindstone in a deepening track.
Which great-grandparent does this child resemble?
Without their history, people stumble
in Triolet, trying not to remember
that they are poor, unalphabeted, black
and historyless. Brown people stumble
along dirt streets, one lost soul to each block.

FOUR

Pray for a God-forsaken Motherland,
a ravished Eden with a thorn-grown gate,
in which the Baobab of Life yet stands.
Pray for a God-forsaken Motherland:
her desert destiny, which seems to end,
but for seeds trusted to the winds of fate.
Pray for our God-forsaken Motherland,
that her seedlings not be crowded out by hate.

FIVE

Our ancestry is ashes on the winds—
the Harmattan, the Khamsin, the Haboob—
blowing from the beginning of the end
of Africa. Blown by her desert winds
blended with the Monsoon, the Bise, the Foehn,
her gene pool, blasted out of solitude.
African slaves were ashes on the winds,
but we survive: one people, many bloods.

SIX

Who talk like me? Who dye elect despise?
Who patois, out day home, invite guffaw
and swallow rage? Mask, except foe day eyes,
who talk like me? Who dye elect despise?
Who teacher strive to you row peonize
dim tongue till day white as you toe pee awe?
Who talk lacking? Who die elect despise?
In a bline whirl, who accent be day flaw?

[handwritten margin note: switch in language when talking about dialect]

SEVEN

Indigenous to no land, only to chance,
despite world history's struggle to weed us out,
we thrive on two seas and three continents.
We are native to no land mass, but chance
makes us one race, heirs of the drum, the dance,
and the cursed blessing of surviving hurt
indigenous to everywhere. Yes, chance
created us, whose ancestors were bought.

EIGHT

The hope of chattels in the barracoons
was that their seed would multiply and spread
around the earth; that even octoroons,
remembering chattels in the barracoons,
would feel sad wonder. *Thy weird will be done,*
they prayed. Whom you gave stones instead of bread.
Yet the faith of chattels in the barracoons
was that you are good and just, and are not dead.

The Cachoeira Tales

Life is nothing but stories.
Albert J. Price, Captain, Ret., American Airlines

General Prologue

When April rains had drenched the root
of what March headlines had foreseen as drought,
I invited my extended family—
with artificial spontaneity—
to join me on some kind of "pilgrimage."
A fellowship gave me the privilege
of offering to cover their airfare
and several nights in a hotel somewhere.
Thinking of a reverse diaspora,
I'd planned a pilgrimage to Africa.
Zimbabwe, maybe, maybe Senegal:
some place sanctified by the Negro soul.

My brother Mel's response was, "What the hey:
I'll go to Timbuktu, if you're going to pay."
My sister Jennifer said, "What's the catch?
It's not like you to offer a free lunch."
I put on my most innocent who-me? look:
No catch. (I planned to use them in this book.)
So she agreed. We vetoed Zimbabwe
because of Mugabe. We couldn't stay,
as I'd hoped, in a village on a farm,
and I might put us in the way of harm
if I took them to the Mizeki Festival,
which honors the black Anglican who fell,
martyred by the spears of his kinspeople.
My option was to fly to Senegal

and visit *L'Abbaye de Keur Moussa.*
I priced a round trip to Dakar: *Py-ha!*
Impossible. Unless we didn't eat . . .
Maybe the monks would put us up gratis . . .
I checked their website. Well, so much for that!
So far, my pilgrimage was falling flat.

I consulted the map: Jamaica? Trinidad?
I'd have to modify the plan I had
concocted on the fellowship application,
but at least we'd have a wonderful vacation.
But, except for visiting Bob Marley's grave
to contemplate his brief, amazing life,
and connecting with Jah in the incense of a joint,
this option offered no apparent point.

Then my son Jacob e-mailed from Brazil,
where he's studying at a Bahian school.
He'd found an inexpensive on-line fare
from L.A., New York, or Miami to Salvador.
We could fly down to Bahia, visit him,
and go to *A Igreja do Bonfim,*
a church on a hill overlooking All Saints' Bay,
sacred to Christians and followers of Candomblé.

We met at JFK. From there we flew
to Salvador together, along with two
other Americans of slave descent.
The following describes the friends who went
together, and the friends we met en route,
simplifying each to a major attribute.

The DIRECTOR of a small black theater
was there. She had decided to be poor,
if that's what it would take to live for art.
She'd spent three decades following her heart's
uncompromisingly high principles,
making aesthetic and political
choices of scripts and casts. For thirty years

stereotypes [handwritten margin note with bracket]

she'd paid her dues to craft and watched her peers
and some less talented become rich shills,
or extras with homes near Beverly Hills
and a taste for cocaine. Her great reviews
didn't increase her theater's revenues:
Black audiences crowded the multiplex,
preferring violence and packaged sex;
white audiences stayed away in droves.
She coveted a car that worked, nice clothes,
and the guilt-free personal luxury.
She could *be* the lipless game-show M.C.
the night the black lady knew the answers,
could *be* George W., in just a couple of glances.
She was an ample sister, middle-aged,
a champagne cocktail of faith and outrage,
with one tooth missing from her ready smile,
a close Afro, and a bohemian style.

A JAZZ MUSICIAN came along as well.
He was the kind of charmer who can sell
drummers insurance. His life's odyssey,
from cutting high school classes regularly
to play the blues, through touring with a band,
through playing for a circus in Japan,
had filled him with good-humored confidence.
In a previous life he might have been a prince,
waving aside the suck-ups and the phonies,
recognized as a man with great *cojones*.
His mother tongue was music: He spoke bass,
flute, and piano, and was of that race
which strives to make work "fit for the plateau."
His California cool, go-with-the-flow
attitude was a most endearing trait,
except that it made him tend to sleep late,
which irritated people less laid-back.
His motto was the universal black
shrug to those who'd make tardiness a crime:
"You have the watches, but we have the time."
He hummed, drummed on tables, and laughed a lot.

you might think you're in control,
but we have the power

13

Thinking of himself as a polyglot
in training, he improvised Portuguese
as he had French, Spanish, and Japanese.
Cigarettes seemed to be his only vice.
But life's a crapshoot played with loaded dice.

The retired PILOT had also held a seat
in the state legislature. A complete
Morehouse man, urbane, witty, and astute,
he had been taught early to elocute
and. he. spoke. clearly. every I.N.G.
He had a deep passion for history,
the disposition of a raconteur,
and the palate of a true connoisseur.
He'd served on the board of the W.C.C.
and was committed to philanthropy.
A worn copy of Emerson's essays
was the last thing he took from his suitcase.
He wore a Greek fisherman's cap and drank
bourbon. He had the dignity of rank
and the habit of looking at his watch,
and when there was no bourbon he drank scotch.
He had eleven siblings, disowned ten,
divorced, and was never married again.
But he'd set his children on the right track:
Both were professionals, proud to be black.
He ordered wine with dinner when he could,
tasting, and then pronouncing it "Damn. Good."

You can spend decades playing by the rules,
counting your blessings, praise in every pulse,
raising your children, making a career,
and have your dearest blessings disappear—
like that. You can tell me it was bum luck
that made a mother stagger thunderstruck
from one hospital bed to the other,
carrying messages between brothers.
But I think God had made another bet,
and won. Maybe God's not satisfied yet

that quality tests of the human soul
have proved the Sixth Day wasn't just a whole
waste of Her precious time, that faith exists
like Job's . . .
             We were joined by an ACTIVIST,
who had been struck by double tragedy
and had broken a killing secrecy
by making "Danny's House" in Washington, D.C.
home to programs on AIDS and HIV.
By serving is one comforted;
by tossing stones into the river's bed
one can change the current of history.
She was planning an autobiography
about the years she spent in the Peace Corps,
about the NAACP and CORE,
about finding her mother . . . I won't paint
the details here. (Her friends say she's a saint.)
And here she was, rediscovering the world:
a certain-age beauty, wide-eyed as a girl.

Now I have thumbnail-sketched the company
of interesting people who went with me,
and who are now (a different now) sitting
around a table, telling sidesplitting
stories, which just unfold in the exchange.
I interrupt, suggesting we arrange
a little competition, with a prize.
Everyone turns, with are-you-kidding? eyes.
Then they turn back, and the pilot tells the rest
of the one about the brother taking the Rorschach test:
"So the shrink says, 'My goodness, Mr. Green,
you have the filthiest mind I've ever seen!'
The brother says, 'It's just like the white man
to blame the Negro! Dr. Smith, you can
say what you want, but you got to admit you're
the one that showed me all them dirty pictures!'"

The Jazz Musician's Tale

At the Modelo market the first day,
Americanos from a mile away,
we were cajoled in the lingua franca:
"Michael Jordan! God bless America!
Sister! Brother! I have good thing for you!"
With prices so low, we couldn't refuse
to play rich for them with our plastic cash.
As we bartered, did scenes from our homes flash
through their minds? Washing machines, dishwashers,
big shiny cars in two-car garages,
computers, Saturdays spent at the malls
buying things we don't need . . .? "Thirty *reais?*"
we said. "Too much. Will you accept eighteen?"
As if those twelve *reais* would strip us clean
and leave us stranded in Brazil. As if
we had to go home to a pregnant wife
and children who are learning how to paint
the pictures tourists take home, of the quaint
cobblestone streets, the salt-bitten pastels
of the *favelas* up there on the hills.

At dinner we agreed about the twerp.
Hasn't anyone else ever heard the word *usurp?*
Finally we approached the subject of race,
and how black skin, in almost every place
we'd traveled, was a liability.
We joked about tickets for D.W.B.
"Speaking of which," the jazz musician said,
"one time I crossed a street against the red
DON'T WALK sign and got thrown in jail.
It was near L.A., in a suburb called Glendale;
I was an hour late, so I ran straight
from my car to the studio across the street.
I had barely touched the curb when a huge roar
skidded up. Man, that cop was mad! He tore
his goggles off, ripped out his book, and leaped
off his bike. He was so pissed off, you'd think

I'd just flipped the bird at the President,
or threatened to bring down the government!
'Do you know what you did?' He jabbed my chest.
'I'm ticketing you!' I wasn't under arrest,
so I took the ticket, apologized, and ran.
And the cop roared off, in search of another black man.

"Two or three years later I was living in L.A.,
picking up gigs wherever I could play.
I finished a gig in Glendale late one night.
I'd just pulled out when a siren and flashing lights
announced cops. Since I'd only had a beer,
I passed the sobriety test. But from the car
the other cop yelled, 'Hey, there's a warrant
on him!' That little jaywalking ticket,
which I'd forgotten about, had grown immense!
Forgetting it was an arrestable offense!
They handcuffed me and threw my ass in jail.
I was there til my mother and my wife came up with the bail.

"With me in the holding tank (it was Saturday night)
were several guys, including a po' white,   *in the same
just out of prison. The first thing he'd done   cell as a
was get himself drunk and kill his woman.   murderer for
A pimp was there, who sort of ministered   j walking*
to everyone; sort of a barrister
without a shingle, he knew the law so well.
He'd talk to everybody, and could tell
you what you needed to do: to pay The Man
or do the time; to get a lawyer when
you had to. He'd gotten this expertise
in several prison-universities.
He was a very good-looking brother
in a green sharkskin suit. Then my mother
steamed in with my wife in her wake, and we
sailed out. It was almost dawn. I was almost free.

"I signed an agreement to appear in court.
It was clear this would only be a short

procedure: I'd just pay the fine and leave.
But the judge said something I couldn't believe:
I'd just explained that I'd been running late,
and that I'd decided I didn't have time to wait,
when the judge asked: 'Why did you cross the street?'
I hesitated for one looooooong heartbeat.
But I couldn't help it; I didn't decide
to answer: 'To get to the other side.'
It just came out! No one in the courtroom laughed.
The gavel slammed down twice. 'Pay the bailiff.'"

The Activist's Tale

"The money of the gringo is the dollar,
the money of the poor is made of copper,"
my son translated from the radio,
singing along with our taxi's chauffeur.
Bicycles, narrow shops, pedestrians
of every shade in the spectrum of bronze,
sun browned, sun blonded, busy with their lives:
to broadcast samba beat, they passed our eyes
as we drove to the ancient pillory,
a living part of Brazil's history,
the square where slaves were tied to posts and flogged.
For years it was left to go to the dogs,
but the last half of the last century
has given it self-respect and tourist money.
Now men there support families on tips
they get from tying ribbons on your wrists.
They smile and shrug when you refuse to pay
after the first dozen. "Okay," they say.
"McDonald's! Coke!" Thumbs up, brown eyes twinkling.

We walked and shopped along, sometimes thinking
about how screams and moans must have been heard
in these cobblestone streets, blood must have flowed
around the cobbles, down the sloping square
of punishment, as if it ran for prayer
to Our Lady of the Rosary of Blacks.
Inside, among the baroque bric-a-brac,
hand-painted signs expressing gratitude
hung on the whitewashed walls: THANK YOU FOR FOOD.
THANK YOU FOR FRIENDS. Almost unbearable,
that brown, black-bearded Jesus, terrible
the burden He must, though He stumble, bear.
How much more poignant He looks with nappy hair.

At dinner we agreed about the rich:
those obscene, greedy children of the Bitch,
who progress, a force with godlike power,

but masterless. "But need is the mother
of invention," the activist went on,
"like that incredible phenomenon,
I don't remember all of the details,
but you know, the man who spent years in a jail
somewhere, with no musical instruments.
He was a white man, but he had some sense:
somehow, he was able to bribe a guard
to bring him paper, pencils, paint, and a board.
He painted eighty-eight black and white keys
and went on to compose several symphonies
which were premiered years later, to acclaim.
I can't quite think of it, but you'd know his name."

Harmonia and Moreen

A man's eyes, when a young Bahiana walks
—saunters? parades? or better: undulates—
when a young Bahiana undulates past him
(back-straight, up-tilting, with sun-gilded limbs
and a butt like twin scoops of *dolce de leite* ice cream)
a man's eyes light up; he snorts puffs of steam.
The old Bahianas, in white eyelet shirts,
the Saints' bright beads, and long white eyelet skirts,
sit by bubbling cauldrons in *acaraje* stands,
scooping shrimp into fritters. With a glance,
men dismiss them; they take a bite and pay.
The old Bahianas watch them walk away.

We heard them first, then met two sisters from home:
Harmonia and her sidekick, Moreen.
They were retracing the diaspora:
they'd just finished doing West Africa;
Jamaica and Haiti were coming next.
Were they wealthy? Or was this the pretext
of two very deep undercover spies?
It might have been a James Bondian disguise.
Just think of the movie possibility:
Two sisters, keeping it safe to be free.
They wore outfits bought on the continent:
Harmonia a turquoise and green print
with matching headwrap, Moreen black and red
with lots of cowries clinking in her dreads.
"You know black people always been wanderers,
but God made us too poor to pay the fare,"
Moreen said, in some kind of secret code
she acted like we were supposed to know.
Harmonia cried, "Yes, girl! That's the truth!"
She poked me with one elbow. "Ain't it the truth?"
Moreen went on: "Negro got put out of line
for first-day gifts at the beginning of time,
because he was looking at White Woman funny.
That's why black folks don't have no money

but we all over the globe. Say amen!
Black folk arrived on the American
part of this planet like seeds riding birds.
Honey, frankly, I wouldn't give two turds
for that piece of desert they fighting about over there.
Somebody need to teach they ass to share!"
Moreen high-fived Harmonia's lifted hand.
"Seem like they need *another* Promised Land!
Seem like some bearded white man with a hat
could prove that if you carefully retranslate
one letter of scripture, you can see God say
the Promised Land's someplace in Uruguay."
Harmonia threw up her hands and screamed.
Then she did a little dance around Moreen.

C.I.A.

Over *moqueca,* rice and beans, we talked
about the narrow winding streets we'd walked,
about shopkeepers waving us to stop,
and how rich we felt walking into a shop
and dropping three dollars for something we loved.
We talked about those Stellas with they groove,
about how friendly the Bahians seemed.
The jazz musician said, "Yet not extreme.
I've witnessed extreme friendliness abroad.
And let me tell you, it was pretty weird.

"My band had booked a gig on a cruise ship,
playing top 40s and getting great tips
for sneaking Sinatra in once in a while.
When we docked, we were free to explore the isle.
I'd walk around, or rent a motorbike,
or if I was feeling ambitious, take a hike.
On every island, once or twice a day,
someone would sidle up to me and say,
'Hello, my brother! (Are you C.I.A.?)'
I'd say I wasn't, and they'd walk away.
By the sixth island, it would have been dense
to think this might be a coincidence.
I asked an asker if he could tell me why
so many people thought I was a spy.
'Aw, Mon,' he said. 'Was you born yesterday?
If you want good dope, you go to the C.I.A.!'
I don't remember that island as well as the rest:
I sold some national secrets and had a blast!"

The Lost Suitcase

Meanwhile, my suitcase hadn't yet arrived;
I'd made do wearing an alternative
wardrobe composed piecemeal of shirts on loan
and underwear dried nightly to the drone
of the hair dryer. My hourly complaints
(which exhibited a saintly self-restraint)
had been translated by the hotel staff,
to no avail: My bag was magicked off.
My son suggested it might be possessed
by the mother of some baggage handler, dressed
like my doppelgänger. He supposed
she might have left an airport in my clothes
and paid sweet promises to get to town.
In the taxi's rearview mirror, he thought, her brown,
loving, all-knowing, all-forgiving eyes
might make the driver immediately recognize
the Saint-ridden woman in the back seat.
Maybe her smile made his heart skip a beat,
then lub-a-dub like the Saint-calling drums
which bring the Saints onto their mediums.
Had he driven her to a *terreiro* to dance
in my white camp shirt and my khaki pants?
Much stranger things have happened in Brazil.
Here, anyone may be someone who will,
on any night, bear a returning soul,
the living self relinquishing control
to be worn, like borrowed clothing, by a Saint.
One grows accustomed to astonishment.
A tethered rooster pecked among the graves
behind the Rosary of Blacks, where slaves
are buried: Some night soon his blood might flow
as offering to those who intercede
between the High God and His children's need.
Did I really need the clothes in that suitcase?
Not if a Saint was wearing them in my place!

Baixa Mall

Our third day promised intermittent showers,
but we're Americans: We can spend hours
in malls, purchasing more of what we have,
on high-interest credit—self-sold slaves
to globalized corporate usury,
chained by ads which insist we're free.
And I *needed* cosmetics, underwear,
a T-shirt. And we *needed* souvenirs . . .
So we took two taxis to the Baixa Mall.
It felt almost like home: the bustling aisles
full of the energy of market day,
vendors marketing wares from far away.
But the trademarks weren't familiar, and the crowds
were every color of the brown rainbow.
And we couldn't believe the low prices:
It was like holding a hand of aces!
The dollar towered over the *real*
like a gun-toting Hollywood cowboy.
The rich must feel like this, spending money
like fountains of beneficence. Honey,
let me tell you, it felt right nice! We ate
in the food court on the Styrofoam plates
we knew from home, though some of the tastes were new.
From the far side of the hall, a loud halloo
called our attention. Harmonia and Moreen!
Moreen in peach, Harmonia in aubergine.
They ran to join us, carrying plastic bags
that slapped against their thighs. "Girl, are we glad
to see y'all!" Harmonia cried. "We loved y'all's plan
to get the Man to move the Promised Land!"
Moreen said, "How about this exchange rate!
I feel like I'm lugging around some great
BIG money! Like the time ol' Anansi
wanted a beautiful woman to see
he was *muy macho,* so he switched his tool
for the tool of his friend, the elephant bull.

Now, you know Trickster's small: He had to haul
that thing around while he waited for the girl.
At first, he let it drag along the ground,
but it hurt, and it tripped him up. He found
it easier to toss it over one shoulder,
though it was like carrying a gold boulder.
When he finally traded back his instrument,
he'd learned something about greed, and good sense.
All this giant money, like a huge tool,
and all them rich people acting the fool
with elephant ding-dongs around their necks,
when a signature on one of their personal checks . . ."
Harmonia cleared her throat and gestured.
"Have you met our guide? I tell you, sisters,
he's the cutest white man I've ever seen!
We have to go." She left, dragging Moreen.

Shrugging, we watched the trio disappear.
What was that gadget in that white man's ear?
We shopped more, then went back to our hotel
to kill some more time checking our e-mail.
Then, after a large meal and the local drink
of rum, sugar, and lemons, still half drunk
with the power of dollars, we relaxed
around a game of conversation catch.
The pilot tossed a high one: During his service
as a board member of the World Council of Churches,
he often traveled on the continent,
and was asked the same two questions wherever he went.
The first question he was asked invariably
was, "You're American? Do you really
have twenty-five different kinds of toothpaste?"
The second, in West Africa or East,
in North or South—and he swore this was true—
was, "Do whites read the same Bible we do?"

"Toothpaste," we echoed. We grew serious,
remembering Africa, which most of us

had visited at least once in our lives.
We sipped our drinks, exchanging narratives:
The director and her daughter taken in,
like long-lost, newfound, much-beloved kin,
by a woman who befriended them in Dakar,
who cooked meals for them on a charcoal fire
behind her house, and pushed the money away
when the director had offered to pay
for her and her family's hospitality.
At last there was an opening for me:
I told about the tranquil week I spent
in the Manger Sisters' Harare convent,
how much I enjoyed kneeling with the nuns
as they prayed the canonical hours with drums.
They fed the poor with produce from their farm
in a remote village. Their order, formed
by a black nun, was all black, one of few
black Catholic religious orders I knew
of, the Oblate Sisters of Providence,
formed in 1829, the oldest.
Its foundress, a free woman, Mother Mary Lange,
was a refugee from the rise of Toussaint
and Haiti's full-blood blacks against the whites
and their mulatto offspring, born of rapes.
Haitian mulatto refugees fled north
and wound up free blacks in the American South,
seventy years before the Civil War.
Mary told her confessor, Père Joubert,
that God was calling her to start a school
and to dedicate her life by taking the veil.
So these should-be candidates for sainthood
collected funds for a girls' school which would
have a curriculum of the classics,
vocational training, art, and music.

Their chapel, not exclusively for blacks,
reserved for their white friends two pews in back.
They took in wash and scrubbed floors on their knees

to take in black orphans and widows. These
domestic talents led their archbishop
to order them to be maids and desist
from the proud sin of thinking they were nuns . . .

The director said, "Is this more of your monk
stuff? Have you been sprinkled with monkey dust,
or something?" She led the laughter of the rest.
(I remembered how I burned her paper dolls;
how I woke up one summer dawn to call,
"It's Christmas!" so she staggered down the stairs
and woke to disappointment and my jeers.
Fifty years later, she's still getting me back
for the way I teased her about her black
favorite doll, which I said was ugly—
or, as we used to say, it was "spoogly"—
"Look at that spoogly ol' black doll!" I'd scream,
with my *Little House* and *Little Women* dreams,
my brain washed white as snow . . .)
                                        But I digress.
Where was I? Oh yes, Africa. The jazz
musician, in Zimbabwe years ago,
was ridiculed because he didn't know
Shona or Ndebele. He was black
so everyone expected him to speak
one of their languages. At last, their fun
made him decide to simply make up one.
"*Uhuru ti matata,*" he said, lifting
his glass to each of them, and then sipping
the local brew. All of the laughers froze.
"What did you say?" they asked. "Oh, you don't know
Swahili," he said, with his eyebrows raised.
"You know Swahili?" They were all amazed,
Swahili being the rough equivalent
of French in Africa. "A dialect,"
he shrugged. "Creole Swahili." They were stunned.
They asked if many black Americans
spoke Swahili. The jazz musician laughed.
"I told them, 'Only in the eastern half

of the country; the rest speak Yoruba.'
They pulled chairs closer and waved to the bar.
'Teach us.' For several hours I drank their beers
and taught them a language invented between my ears."

*Monk's
Tale?*

My son said that Bahians know the tribes
of their ancestors and have kept alive,
in chants, phrases, and words, the languages
they prayed in during the Middle Passage.
Their gods survived by putting on white masks,
so slaves could answer, when their masters asked,
"We pray, as you have taught us, to the One,
to His white saints, and to His Jewish son."

The Christian saints became the Orixas:
Yemanja-Mary, Oxala-Jesus . . .
Or was it vice versa? We paused to think,
meanwhile ordering another round of drinks—
two lemons squeezed, a scoop of sugar, rum,
shaken, not stirred, served over ice—and *yum!*
We drew near the point of feeling no pain.
The ball fell in the pilot's court again.
He told about flying into a coup
somewhere: I think it was Ouagadougou.
He was ordered to taxi to the gate,
keep the doors locked, take no pictures, and wait.
He shoved his camera underneath his seat
and sat there sweltering in the tropical heat.
Whose funds paid for those guns? He didn't care;
all he wanted was his butt back in the air.
Aloft again, after hours of red tape,
he thought, "Thank God my ancestors escaped."

The bar man brought another round of drinks
and cleared away the empties. Were those winks
between him and the pilot? Possibly.
The jazz musician's volubility
took great leaps forward. Here and there, a word

was garbled, consonants were slurred.
We talked about bureaucracy and greed,
rampant corruption, bribes, visible need,
the land's intractability, the snakes,
the ignorance, the beauty, how dawn breaks
on people already up and about,
how the full moon rises over the veldt.
I met a young woman near Victoria Falls,
one morning on my constitutional,
a basket on her head, her baby tied high
so it peeked over her shoulder. Her eyes,
as we approached each other, watched the road.
My spoken greeting startled her; her load
slipped off her head. I saw, in slow motion,
her momentary loss of composure:
she turned to catch it, and the baby fell,
headfirst, out of its sling. Some miracle
made it fall right into my hands. I felt
like Holden Caulfield, in spite of my guilt—
for I'd averted a near-tragedy,
which almost happened, almost caused by me.
That woman's humble, wet-eyed gratitude
couldn't convince me I'd done something *good.*

The activist asked, "What about those nuns?
Did Mother Mary Lange stick by her guns?
Did lightning strike the bishop? I won't sleep
a wink tonight, unless I know what hap-
pened." I told her she was obedient.
Seeing the bishop's order as expedient,
she and her sisters hired out as maids.
The earnings from their cleaning service paid
to keep widows and orphans housed and fed,
and they held school at night. When Mary died,
they knew she was one of the Ancestors.
"How come she's not a saint?" asked the director.
The jazz musician said, "She is." He yawned.
"I'm bushed. Okay, let's have a show of hands:

who's for hitting the sack, and sleeping in
tomorrow? I could use a vacation
from my vacation: Gimme some time to chill!"
We acquiesced. Good night, sleep tight, Brazil.

Through the Wormhole

I was alone on a cobblestone street,
rushing to the place I'd been told I'd meet
the tall, dark, handsome stranger of my dreams,
when I heard the far whispering of drums.
So faint, so faint, as faint as a heartbeat,
they called, in words I knew. I told my feet
to do their stuff, running past closed blue doors,
not away from, but toward a universe
I knew awaited me through the wormhole
I'd fall into when a door in a white wall
swallowed me, like a Wonderland cliché.
So faint, so faint, the drums. And then I lay,
surrounded by the drumming of bare feet,
in a room scented with incense and sweat.
The drums, the drums throbbed in my arteries,
calling again onto living bodies
the Holy Ones who answer to black names.
Ka-doom. Ka-doom, doom, doom. They came,
as they have come for untold centuries,
to ride the bodies of their devotees,
crossing the threshold between here and God.
Mounted, I felt my identity fade,
a star on the horizon of true self.
Another I takes flesh, another will,
in this steed I control with gentle reins,
to speak for me. My name is . . .
                                    The phone rang.
It was the desk: My suitcase had been found.
I tipped the bellman, locked the door, lay down
in bed again, then jumped back up to pee.
What should be made of this ability
our people seem to have, of mediumhood?
I checked the mirror, and went back to bed.
Can rational science explain the gift
of being ridden, being spirit-possessed?
Is it mumbo-jumbo mysticism,
or a true path rejected by racism?

What do the gods say? I thought thoughts like these,
and those . . . and theys . . . And then I piled up Zs.
I need to pick up something at the store . . .
I need to pick up something at the store . . .
I need to pick up something at the store . . .
I enter through the automatic door,
steer past the florist, deli, bakery,
fish market, butcher, and greengrocery,
putting things in my cart, wondering why
the world is so screwed up. In the Big Y
I find my weekly respite from the news.
Strolling along its glistening avenues,
humming along to denatured pop songs,
no news, no news, as long as I buy things
and leaf through tabloids in the cashier's line.
No news, no news, an hour in the clean,
noon-bright, odorless, disinfected air.
No news of the madness raging out there.
Cereals, miles of plastic and cardboard
packaging, and a spotless floor,
and other shopping zombies, in a kind
of walking meditation, focused mind:
I need to pick up something from the store . . .
I need to pick up something from the store . . .
No news, no traces of insects or mice,
a world of one-way traffic, and of nice,
mostly white, smiling neighbors. And no news.
I muse along, silently psalmodize,
ask God, or Big Mama, to pull us through.
Opening a glass door, I reach into
the low-calorie, fat-free frozen treats,
and a swirling funnel of light and heat
sucks me breathlessly to the other side.
Where am I? Harmonia and Moreen's guide
is talking to his watch, looking at me.
I know they *know.* They know I've secretly
incited riots in my fantasies,
fomented revolutions. He begins
to walk toward me. I turn on my heels and run

along a narrow, fly-filled corridor,
wheelbarrows, carts, stands, tables, disorder,
brown people selling things and buying them,
lightbulbs, electronics. I can see him
pushing people aside in calm pursuit.
I dodge between vegetables and fruits,
tables displaying bundles of dried leaves,
tables displaying chunks of bloody meat,
into an odorific aisle of fish,
and human victims, bombed pieces of flesh,
I'm running, running, horror-struck.
I'm running, running, through the thick
carrion song of flies, to save
people, to keep people alive.
The buzz ascends to join the roar of planes
aimed at a tower made of people's names.
"No, wait!" I scream, trapped in a labyrinth,
the narrowing gyre of a labyrinth,
screaming. I run, heart pounding with terror,
chased to the dark heart of human error,
where a man sits praying a one-way prayer
and plotting new ways to create horror.

He opens his eyes, smiles at me. I scream,
"You're something I ate! You're just a fucking dream!"

Southern Cross

I slept through the hotel's breakfast buffet
and took my headache out into a day
brilliant with noon reflected off the waves
and freshened by a redolent sea breeze.
The activist waved from the esplanade,
wearing her baseball cap. I thought, *Oh God,
this means I'll have to get some exercise.*
My good angel began to sermonize
about the benefits of a brisk walk;
her brother, still strengthened by alcohol,
brokered the compromise of a slow stroll
with a good opportunity to talk.
They said, "And to catch stories!" and slapped palms.
It's not often those two work as a team.
The director came out just as the light went green,
and we three women set out on our own.
Below us, people eddied on the beach,
some walking, some bathing, some stopped to watch
young people practice *capoeira* kicks.
A martial art as graceful and complex
as tai chi, self-defense disguised as dance,
this is another slave inheritance.
Beyond the growing circle of applause
mothers chatted on towels, children splashed;
lovers rubbed sunscreen on each other's backs;
lovers held hands . . . I wax elegiac,
trying to describe the unsayable.
Sometimes beauty is inconveyable,
except in the one syllable of *ah!*
Imagine a moment when there's no war
anywhere on earth, when no one dies
of violence or hunger, when the wise
are listened to: The beach scene was like that.
I thought to myself, *How lucky can you get?
As the pilot says, "Life is good,* so far."
Here we were in the Southern Hemisphere,

among people who might be relatives,
beside the burial place of millions of slaves.
The blue Atlantic smiles. Below its mask,
a bone highway, waters salted with flesh.
The Orixas followed that skeletal road
to bring their solace, and to intercede
with the infinite overarching Force
who blessed history with history's curse
to dress these crowds in their New World brown skin,
blood of three continents. Soaking up sun,
children and grandmothers, modest and thonged:
beautiful blessings, engendered by wrong.

In front of one of the nicer hotels
a large, prawn-pink blond man immersed himself.
Never have I seen a less preening beach,
a less abashed. I suddenly sensed that each
of these sun-worshippers knew that a soul
resides in every body. On a hill
jagged as a stone molar, we sat down
on a bench at the base of the lighthouse.
For how many centuries of nights
has its Morse code of reassuring light
pulsed toward Angola? Here at its stone foot
we watched in silence, then began to shoot
the breeze. The activist, glowing with love
she'd long ago stopped hoping for, told of
defending her two sons from homophobes
who thought their sexuality defined
them, who thought they had AIDS because they'd sinned.
She spoke of being blamed, of being shunned
while she was the mother of dying sons,
like other AIDS mothers around the world,
helplessly watching little boys and girls
grow up to die of unprotected love.
We sat a long time, watching the blue waves.
The director had a friend who moved away
because he was ashamed of being gay
and sick. When his friends found him, he was close

to death in a hotel room, comfortless.
They took turns flying out to be with him,
their love unchanged, his secret safe with them.
We talked of the greed of drug companies
who want a profit to cure miseries,
who are letting Africa die for lack of cash,
while all the West will do is stand and watch.
We sat a long time, watching the wide waves.
Little fish and big fish, have-nots and haves.
We bought American canned sodas from
a burdened woman who opened them with her thumb
and handed them to us with humble thanks.
She stood aside waiting as we drank,
then took our empties. The world was too much
with us. We rose and walked back down the beach.

Like a linen armada on a sea
of bared, browned, beautiful anatomies,
we set sail toward the granite rendering
of Jesus on a stony outcropping
which towered like a prow over flung spume.
We knew Him from afar by His costume:
the drapery of robes down to His feet,
His long, straight hair. He waved, as if to greet
His namesake city, or as if He blessed,
in the name of His Father, all who passed.

We stopped below His sandals and looked down
on the Bay of All Saints, and on their town.
"I wonder if He finds any wisdom
in New World African syncretism,"
the activist mused. The director said,
"Aren't all religions, finally, homebred?
If Jesus had been born an Eskimo,
lost souls would be lost seals. The way you know
if what people believe holds any truth
is to watch how they live. That's where the proof
of the pudding is. Anyway, that's what
I think. How 'bout you, St. Magnificat?"

I waited until I'd counted to ten
and my good angel started to kick in.
Then I blah-blahed about theology:
inculturation; the reality
the icon points to, the symbolic truth
visible through it to the eyes of faith;
the incarnation of the avatar,
the bodhisattva; eternal Buddha
and historical Buddha; cosmic Christ
and Jesus. I began to make a list
of saints and avatars. When we pray to
St. Francis, for example, we pray through
that wonderful man to the God he praised,
I said. Perhaps the Orixas are doorways
to Divine Presence. "He who loves the moon,"
I quoted at them, "also loves the sun."
I told about my visit to Meera,
recognized early as an avatar
of God's female face, in her German home.
I knelt with others, waiting for my turn
to kneel at her knees, look into her eyes.
I told them she looked beautiful and wise,
that she looked deep into me, with a gaze
that felt like true love, that I sometimes raise
a prayer to her. I don't believe it hurts.
After all, God hears any prayer God wants
to hear. Then I recounted how my son,
in a front-seat to back-seat discussion,
once laid all my theology to waste
by asking, "How can God be in toothpaste?"

Da Blues

We spent the afternoon just lying low,
preparing for the party we would throw
that evening, for my son's friends, at a jazz
club, so his Brazilian friends could meet his
"illustrious" family. He had arranged
dinner before it opened, and the stage
before the paid band came, so his uncle
and his musician friends could jam until
the club opened. The jazz musician said
he had to spend some time inside his head.
So a quick lunch, then quiet. In our room
we drew the drapes and listened to the hum
of air conditioning. It was a surf
on the island where Snook discovered truth . . .
I dreamed about a little marooned dog
who prayed to his master, as to a god
who loved him and was trying to return
to rescue him. Meanwhile Snook (the dog) learned
compassion for all sentient beings' pain.
A Master now, when he was found again
he wagged his tail and yapped. I woke refreshed.
The director and I showered and got dressed.
In the lobby we met up with the rest,
then we taxied off to Show Time and our guests.
My fellowship allowed me to invite
thirty to a choice of three meals, either white
or red wine, water, or soft drinks or beer.
My son walked around grinning ear to ear,
translating, introducing: a fine host
to the Brazilians who mattered the most
to him in Salvador. Professors, friends,
kids from the poetry program where he spends
some hours every week, the elegant,
famous artist friend of a friend . . . I can't
remember everyone. Someone who'd known
Jorge Amado . . . Some American
students, like my son studying abroad . . .

The "program" began with a spoken-word
performance by two kids from the program.
I couldn't understand, but what aplomb
they showed! Walking among the tables, they
addressed lines to us individually
and called lines to each other, poetry
bringing us into a community.

They sat down to applause. *Sotto voce,*
the jazz musician said, "Before I play,
I like to think of my first time on skis.
From the ski lift I looked down onto trees
and up to snow and an astounding sky.
When we got off, my buddy shouted, 'Bye!'
and whizzed away. I stood a second, stunned,
then shoved off like a bullet from a gun.
I kept my balance with the poles, and flew
straight down the mountain. I didn't know what to do
to slow down or to stop. Faster and faster
I swooshed, heading right into disaster:
Someone fell down a couple of hundred yards
ahead of me. I closed my eyes, prayed hard,
and, visualizing an Olympic ski jumper,
lifted my ski tips and leaped into the air.
And time stood still, for one long, soaring breath,
as I transcended injury or death.

"Jazz is like that." He sat at the keyboard,
nodded to the young musicians, and soared.

Thirty minutes into the improvised
jazz standards, solos played with undisguised
delight on the keyboard, drums, guitar, and bass,
a loud noise interrupted the smooth grace
of "Night in Tunisia," and who appeared,
gaudy as two Amazonian birds,
but long-lost Moreen and Harmonia.
Moreen cried, "Yes, they here! Hallelujah!
Two *caipirinhas,* please." When their drinks came

we reentered the meditative calm
of hearing notes played once in a lifetime
in a wordless striving to reach the sublime,
to disappear into a melody
until the music is the harmony
of stars and planets. Then the hired band
took over, and the regular guests began
to fill the room. The female vocalist
sang Jobim nicely, and we ate the rest
of our dinners and ordered another round
of drinks. The band had perfected a sound
we knew from grocery store Muzak:
pretty, but lacking passion, too laid-back.
We clapped. Time passed. We clapped. They left the stage.
Then "our" musicians, drunk with beverage
and fellowship, asked in English, "The Blues?"
The jazz musician shrugged, "Who could refuse
this opportunity? Okay, niños,
let's boogie!" They played until the club closed.

My brother gave them the chords and snapped a beat
until the others nodded their complete
nonverbal understanding. Then they launched
one Blues after another, with the raunch
of a nightclub on Chicago's South Side
in the fifties. My brother closed his eyes,
burned up the keys, and sang like one possessed
by Maceo Merryweather or Leroy Carr.
He sang, *Ain't gonna be a fool no more,*
and *Couldn't make the payments,* and *You gone.*
Tunes melted into new tunes, in a long
repertoire I'd had no idea he knew.
My baby bro' a master of the Blues!
Mama would have been proud. *Yes, I was born,*
he sang, *with a forehead ready to frown.*
My sister whispered, "He's making these up."
The guests on the far side of the nightclub
clapped and emitted whistles, moans, and screams.
People put little notes among the flames

rising from the keyboard. Harmonia
jumped up and threw her hands into the air.
Wiggling her large, orange-clad derriere,
she danced like a bride's mother in Ghana.

The kitchen staff came out, as the Blues flew
from one pair of feet to another. Few
managed to sit out the cyclone of joy
contained in the music of black despair.
Few managed not to moan, or to shout *YES!*
to the recitation of the ills the flesh
is heir to, which makes your feet go one way
and your backside another. Do we pray
when we dance with our hands over our heads?
He sang, *My baby left, and took the bed!*

Three hundred dollars paid for thirty meals
with beverages, and for the alcohol
and soft drinks our group drank, the evening through.
Three hundred dollars. I paid the musicians, too:
a good amount there; in New York a tip
to make a taxi driver curl his lip,
say thanks sarcastically, and squeal away.
They thanked me profusely. What could I say?
The evening cost about what I'd have paid
for two, for an equivalent soiree
in Manhattan. My brother hugged "his band."
We snagged a taxi home to slumberland.

Music Monastery

Driving through Salvador's wee-hour streets,
past hotels, shops, apartments (through red lights),
the Bluesman said, "They say there is a place
a few musicians in a genera-
tion get into: A music monastery,
very ascetic, very strict, very,
very selective. Few people apply,
'cause if you get rejected: Man, you *die!*"
The director laughed, and I pooh-poohed his facts,
but it proved impossible to distract
him from his story, which he claimed was true.
Though, when we pressed, he said nobody knew
where it was. "In Nepal, maybe; or Tibet.
Someplace with mountains, someplace you can't get
ten radio stations playing the Top Ten
same tunes around the clock. The regimen
of deprivation and practice is known
only by those Masters who graduate.
They are the musicians the world knows as *great.*
They say Ornette Coleman was lost for years;
even his family thought he'd disappeared.
He reappeared wearing the saffron robe
of the Highest Master. And his music awed
the music world."
                              In front of our hotel
the sound of surf drew us into its spell.
We walked down the beach, carrying our shoes,
around a floodlit soccer match. The Blues
sang in our silence. Wading in the waves,
I thought of Matthew Arnold. Then, of slaves.
I sat on a stone, lost in revery,
and watched my siblings walk into the sea.

The hotel staff didn't seem to be nonplussed
by their crazy, sopping-wet American guests.

In Memoriam:

Benjamin O. Davis (1912–2002)
and Bertram W. Wilson (1922–2002)

Late morning e-mails brought news of the deaths
of B. O. Davis, and my dear friend Bert.
Two great Tuskegee Airmen bite the dirt.
Shaken, I followed an internet path
through websites devoted to Candomblé,
wiping away an occasional slow tear.
I read about possession by lesser spir-
its: Indians, old black people. Some play
as children, making faces, begging for treats.
The dance seems to release the essential myth
sacred to every tribe, of a deathless Self.
How grief recedes, faith dawns, faced with such sweet
assurances of immortality.
Colonel Wilson, General Davis: Live in me.

Olodum

"Where there is dancing, there is hope."

Jake had to take some books back up to CRIA,
where teens study Brazilian *poesía*
and read bits of translated poetry.
(The apple didn't fall far from the tree.)
And Olodum was playing later that night;
we shouldn't miss them: They were dynamite,
he said. So, in the middle afternoon,
we rode to Pelhourino. Olodum,
a band of drummers, was an important part
of that section's renewal, using art
as a hammer to reshape poverty
into a thriving tourist industry.
We walked again along the treeless streets,
past vendors of souvenirs, ribbons, gum, sweets,
and fragrant *acaraje*. Musicians played;
youths performed *capoeira*. Our parade
of tourist dollars was welcomed again
by vendors who remembered us as friends:
"My friends!" they called in English; "I love you!"
We spent more money. What else can you do?
We sought refuge in the St. Francis church,
whose gilt interior invited us to search
for gargoyle-cherubs angry slaves had carved
for lazy, fat-cat Christians, while they starved.
Some are still grimacing. But the hard-ons
the guidebooks mentioned all seemed to be gone.
The activist suggested daintily
that a restroom was needed urgently.

We hastened out to search for a café.
The director told a story on the way:
"This friend of mine told me she had to pee
immediately, once, while she was ski-
ing down a Colorado mountainside.
She had to go so badly, she decid-
ed to pull over in a clump of pines

and do her thing. She skied to the tree line,
hid, lowered her pants, and squatted. As she sighed
two relieved clouds of steam, she started to slide
backwards, out of the trees. She couldn't stop;
she skied up a large mogul. In the drop-
off coming down the other side, she fell
and sprained her knee. The vigilant ski patrol
travoised her to a waiting ambulance.
Supine, she struggled to pull up her pants,
wondering why they were just idling there.
Some time later, the ski patrol reappeared
with a young man who had broken his arm.
After they'd gotten him settled and warm,
as they sirened down the curvaceous mountain road,
she asked him how he'd fallen. He replied
that a bare-assed woman skiing backward
had sped toward him; in order to avoid
colliding with this sight beyond belief,
he'd swerved without looking, and hit a tree."

We took turns. Then we took turns ordering
our dinners: Wine, of course, and rice and beans,
Brazil's famous *feijoada*. As we raised
our glasses to the pilot's nightly praise—
"Well, the trip has been great, *so far*"—we heard
a familiar commotion, and the birds
of paradise were borrowing two chairs
from other tables, to pull up to ours.
"You all certainly do know how to throw
a party," said Harmonia. Closing
her eyes, raising her hands, for once Moreen
seemed speechless, momentarily. We ate;
they ordered, waited, said grace over their plates,
and joined the general gusto. "Lord, these beans
are better than my mama's," said Moreen.
"I eat them every chance I get. Too bad
ol' ass can't whistle." After we'd ha-ha'd,
she added, "Of course, y'all know why it can't.
. . . How can y'all be black, and so ignorant?"

Miller's Tale?

(I thought, "Good question!") "Well," she said, "I'll tell
you, since you asked. It was during a spell
of bad hunting. Trickster shot a gazelle
at the end of another hungry day.
He made a fire, spitted the meat, and lay
with his back to the fire, to take a nap.
He told his ass to stay awake, keep watch,
and whistle a warning if it saw a thief.
Then Trickster closed his eyes and fell asleep.
A jackal skulked out of a nearby bush.
The ass whistled. It fled. Trickster said, 'Hush!
Ain't nothing there!' And he went back to sleep.
Two jackals came. The ass whistled: 'Peep! Peep!'
They fled. Trickster woke up. 'I told you, *hush!*
Ain't nothing there!' His breath became the shush
of sleep again. Three jackals. The ass peeped.
Trickster awoke, furious, out of deep sleep,
and looked around. 'You *double-expletive* liar!'
he yelled, 'Take *this!*' And he sat down in the fire,
to punish ass for crying wolf. Poor ass
got badly burnt. That's how it come to pass
that ass can't whistle. When it tries . . ." Moreen
puckered her lips. We roared like libertines.

The enclosed plaza where Olodum plays
was crammed with colors, from café au lait
to Hershey's Kisses (trademark), and pigs' feet,
a crowd that overflowed into the street
and down the block. The only tickets left
were sold by scalpers guilty of horse theft
with their outrageous prices. But we paid,
to be shoehorned in and gallimaufried.
Joined skin to skin,we moved like molecules
in the great, impossible miracle
of atmosphere, swaying to the music,
all eyes on the stage, all hearts attuning
themselves in beautiful polyrhythmy,
one shaking booty. On one side of me
a young man danced; I felt his muscled warmth

Miller's Tale?

flow into mine, his pure, sexual strength.
On my other sides young women danced, whose curves
bumped me softly, dancing without reserve,
hands waving in the air, releasing scent
fragrant as nard. We danced in reverent,
silent assent to the praise-song of drums.
The singers sang in Portuguese, but one
repeated English phrase I understood:
"If Jesus were a black man . . ." In the crowd,
one molecule remembered a long, loud,
sixties party, where several of her friends
from different African countries took turns
playing a Quaker's Oatmeal box, surprised
that the rhythms meant the same things to their tribes.
The drums talk. Is there no Rosetta Stone
by which to translate their names for the One
whose dark faces mask Divine Radiance?
I thought I understood, then: They said *Yes.*
God doesn't prefer one language, one gesture,
one form of prayer, one praying posture;
God doesn't prefer the ascetic's self-denial
to the delighted joy-dance of the child.
Half of the families in Brazil earn less
than $4,000 a year. There are estimates
that eight to ten million children live in the street.
Yes, say the drums; *yes,* say the hips and feet,
dancing to sacred music. Levity
celebrates life's one-drumbeat brevity—

Cachoeira

We slept, woke, breakfasted, and met the man
we'd hired as a tour guide, with a van
and driver, for the day. We were to drive
to Cachoeira, where the sisters live:
the famous Sisterhood of the Good Death,
founded by former slaves in the nineteenth
century. "Negroes of the Higher Ground,"
they called themselves, the governesses who found-
ed the Sisterhood as a way to serve the poor.
Their motto, *"Aiye Orun,"* names the door
between this world and the other, kept ajar.
They teach that death is relative: We rise
to dance again. Locally canonized,
they lead quiet, celibate, nunnish lives,
joining after they've been mothers and wives,
at between fifty and seventy years of age:
a sisterhood of sages in matronage.

We drove on Salvador's four-lane boulevards,
past unpainted cement houses, and billboards,
and pedestrians wearing plastic shoes,
and little shops, and streets, and avenues,
a park, a mall . . . Our guide was excellent:
fluent in English, and intelligent,
willing to answer questions patiently
and to wait out our jokes. The history
of Salvador flew past. At Tororo
we slowed as much as the traffic would allow,
to see the Orixas dancing on the lake
in their bright skirts. The road we took
sped past high-rise apartment neighborhoods,
then scattered shacks, then nothing but deep woods
of trees I didn't recognize and lands
that seemed to be untouched by human hands.
We stopped in a village, where it was market day.
We walked among the crowds, taller than they
and kilos heavier, tasting jackfruit

[handwritten margin note:] aiye = physical   orun = spiritual

and boiled peanuts, embraced by absolute,
respectful welcome, like visiting gods
whose very presence is good news. Our guide
suggested a rest stop. We were sipping Coke
when a man came into the shop and quietly spoke
to our guide, who translated his request:
Would we come to his nightclub, be his guests?
We didn't understand, but shrugged and went
a few doors down the street. "What does he want?"
we asked. The club hadn't been opened yet;
by inviting us in, the owner hoped to get
our blessings for it. Which we humbly gave:
visiting rich American descendants of slaves.

For hours we drove through a deep wilderness,
laughing like children on a field-trip bus.
We made a side trip to the family home
of Bahia's favorite daughter and son,
the Velosos, Bethania and Caetano,
in the small town of Santo Amaro.
The greenery flew by until the descent
into a river valley. There we went
to a nice little restaurant to dine
on octopus stew, rice, manioc, and wine.
Then we crossed a rickety bridge behind a dray
drawn by a donkey, and wended our way,
at last, to Cachoeira, an old town
of colonial buildings, universally tan
and shuttered, darkly lining narrow streets.
A tethered rooster pecked around our feet
in the souvenir shop. At the convent
I wondered what the statues really meant:
Was it Mary, or was it Yemanja
in the chapel, blue-robed, over the altar?
Was it Mary on the glass-enclosed bier,
her blue robe gold-embroidered, pearls in her hair,
or was it the Orixa of the sea?
There were no Sisters around for us to see;
they were in solitude, preparing for the Feast

of the Assumption, when the Virgin passed
painlessly from this world into the next,
Aiye to *Orun*. Posters showed them decked
out for their big Assumption Day parade,
big, handsome mamas wearing Orixa beads,
white turbans and blouses, red shawls, black skirts.
The man in their gift shop was an expert
on the Sisters' long struggle to find a way
to serve the Christian Church and Candomblé.
The eldest Sister is called "the Perpetual Judge";
every seventh year, she becomes the bridge
on which the Virgin Mary crosses back,
sorrowing love incarnate in a black
ninety-odd-year-old woman facing death
and saying *Magnificat* with every breath.

We drove out of the valley looking back
on lightbulbs which intensified the thick,
incomprehensible, mysterious
darkness of the unknown. Grown serious
and silent in our air-conditioned van,
we rode back into the quotidian.

A Igreja do Nostra Senhor do Bonfim

Bags packed, my siblings agreed to squeeze in,
to shut me up, a trip to the Bonfim
Church, though we might need a police escort
with sirens to get us to the airport
to make our flight back to the U.S.A.
The pilot and the activist would stay
in the hotel until their Rio plane.
So we four set off, to fulfill the plan
for which I'd won my fellowship. The man
who drove our taxi understood our need:
Instead of taking major roads whose speed
was slowed by rush-hour traffic, he cut through
the neighborhoods where tourists seldom go.
Clusters of uniformed children walked to school.
Workers waited for buses, crisp and cool-
looking. (They'd come home wilted by the heat,
after a day of smiling.) Every street
we drove on or caught glimpses of was clean.
Shopkeepers unlocked doors, and laid out green
vegetables and many colors of fruit.
I thanked God we'd been forced to take this route,
to look into open windows and doors.
This was a world we would not have explored,
a world with no neon and no street lights,
a world which makes tourists feel discrete fright,
"But I'm not racist; one of my best friends . . ."
I told them about the time my eyes were cleansed.

I'd gone to Mexico, on sort of a whim,
to join a week-long seminar program
offered by the Sisters of Guadalupe.
I'd gone alone, but was there with a group
of gringo students and their chaperones.
My reason for being there wasn't entirely known
to them or me. Especially to me.
It stemmed more from *eros* than from *agape*.
We breakfasted in silence every day,

then met in the sunny oratory to pray.
They prayed. I gazed out over the landscape:
a steep arroyo and a barren sweep
of sagebrush and cactus. Our days were spent
on lectures about poverty. Or we went
into the homes of the hospitable poor.
We sat on their up-turned pail furniture,
exchanged life stories and farewell blessing.
Each day more humbled by our possessing
so much of the earth's power, I felt sad
and powerless. Late in the week we made
a trek to an arroyo, down and out,
and across land caught in a perpetual drought.
We followed a mile-long extension cord
to a village built of tin and billboards,
where chickens, dogs, and children ran in the dust.
The Sisters greeted people, introduced
their visitors, inquired about health
and gardens. I experienced my wealth
acutely, painfully. At evensong
I saw, where I'd been gazing all along,
that village: right there, in front of my eyes.
I, who had been blind, could now recognize
the individual homes of people I'd met.
That was an awakening I shall not forget.

At the church, descended upon by a swarm
of vendors, we showed the ribbons on our arms
and, shaking our heads to trinkets, rushed inside
to see the room described in all the guides:
walls festooned with emblems of prayers answered.
Snapshots of people who've survived cancer,
unneeded crutches . . . An awesome display.
Then I rushed into the sanctuary to pray,
quickly, that all of us would meet good ends.
I turned: My brother signaled with one hand;
we ran back to our taxi. As we sped
down highways toward the airport, my son said,
"The Lord of Bonfim is both Oxala,

a long-ago king in West Africa,
and Christ. One day Oxala put on rags
to disguise himself, and went with a bowl to beg.
He hoped to see how his people lived, to find
and scourge the cruel, and reward the kind.
Arrested for vagrancy, he was thrown in jail.
Not knowing where he was, no one brought bail.
He sat for years in solitude and filth,
meditating on poverty and wealth.
At last his son Oxossi happened to pass
the miserable jail and see Oxala's face.
His long-lost father, given up for dead!
The king lives! Oxala was quickly freed
and, bathed with honors, returned to his throne.
He said, 'I have learned with my flesh and bones
the conditions under which my people live.
The waters which bathed me are going to give
comfort to those who suffer, and to quench
the fires of greed, injustice, and violence.'
From that day forth, Oxala's kingdom thrived;
he was known as the wisest king who ever lived.
There's a huge procession once a year to wash,
with scented water, the steps of the church,
in honor of Oxala and his twin,
the Christian Christ: both Lords of the Good End."

Our pilgrimage ended, we left Salvador.
Meanwhile, our President cheered us toward war—